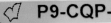

Henry Ford

by Jonatha A. Brown
Reading consultant: Susan Nations, M.Ed., author/literacy coach/consultant

WR WEEKLY READER
EARLY LEARNING LIBRARY

Please visit our web site at: www.earlyliteracy.cc
For a free color catalog describing Weekly Reader® Early Learning Library's list
of high-quality books, call 1-877-445-5824 (USA) or 1-800-387-3178 (Canada).
Weekly Reader® Early Learning Library's fax: (414) 336-0164.

Library of Congress Cataloging-in-Publication Data

Brown, Jonatha A.
    Henry Ford / by Jonatha A. Brown.
      p. cm. — (People we should know)
    Includes bibliographical references and index.
    ISBN 0-8368-4466-1 (lib. bdg.)
    ISBN 0-8368-4473-4 (softcover)
    1. Ford, Henry, 1863–1947—Juvenile literature. 2. Automobile industry and trade—
United States—Biography—Juvenile literature. 3. Industrialists—United States—
Biography—Juvenile literature. 4. Automobile engineers—United States—Biography—
Juvenile literature. I. Title. II. Series.
    TL140.F6B775   2004
    338.7'6292'092—dc22
    [B]   2004057439

This edition first published in 2005 by
Weekly Reader® Early Learning Library
330 West Olive Street, Suite 100
Milwaukee, WI 53212 USA

Copyright © 2005 by Weekly Reader® Early Learning Library

Based on *Henry Ford* (Trailblazers of the Modern World series) by Michael Burgan
Editor: JoAnn Early Macken
Designer: Scott M. Krall
Picture researcher: Diane Laska-Swanke

Photo credits: Cover, title, pp. 4, 19 © Hulton Archive/Getty Images; pp. 5, 9, 10, 12, 16, 17, 21
From the Collections of Henry Ford Museum and Greenfield Village; p. 7 © General Photographic
Agency/Getty Images; p. 11 © Keystone Features/Getty Images; p. 14 © Spencer Arnold/Getty Images

Printed in the United States of America

1 2 3 4 5 6 7 8 9 09 08 07 06 05

Table of Contents

Words that appear in the glossary are printed in **boldface**
type the first time they occur in the text.

Chapter 1: Farm Boy

When Henry was young, horses and carts filled the roads.

Henry Ford was born on July 30, 1863. He lived in Dearborn, Michigan. He grew up in a time that was very different from our own. There were no electric lights in those days. There were only gas lamps and candles. There were no telephones. Horses pulled carts on the streets. Trains carried people from town to town. Travel was slow.

The Ford family lived on a farm. Henry was the oldest of six children. He grew up knowing how hard farmers worked. As a boy, Henry did not like farm work. He liked machines. He thought people should use machines to do the hard work on a farm.

Henry was a **curious** boy. When he was young, he wanted to know how all

Henry was not quite three years old in this picture.

sorts of things worked. He took wind-up toys apart to see how they were built. He wanted to see what made them move.

Soon he began to build small machines of his own. He and some friends made a little mill. It worked well enough to grind potatoes and dirt. Later, Henry and his friends built a small **steam engine**. That machine did not work. In fact, it blew up! The flying metal cut Henry, but being hurt did not stop him. He kept right on building little machines.

A New Kind of Machine

When he was twelve, Henry saw a machine he had never seen before. It was a new kind of cart. Horses did not pull this cart. Instead, a steam engine made it move. Burning coal kept the engine running.

This fire engine was used in the late 1800s. It was powered by steam.

Henry was surprised. He ran to see the cart. He wanted to know all about the cart and its engine. The driver explained how they worked. Then he let the boy run the engine. Henry never forgot the thrill he felt that day.

Chapter 2: Engineer

When he was sixteen years old, Henry moved to Detroit. There he found a job as an **engineer**. He worked with steam engines. Even though he was young, he was good at running and fixing engines. He liked his job more than farm work.

Steam Engines on Farms

Henry returned home in 1882. By then, farmers were using steam engines. They supplied power to grind grain, cut corn, and saw wood. Henry had no trouble finding jobs. He went from farm to farm and worked on steam engines.

Henry liked to think of new uses for engines. He had some good ideas. One was to use an engine to run a tractor. But steam engines were not very safe. They could explode if they were not handled right.

At twenty-three, Henry was already thinking about building a gas-powered car.

Henry began to think about gas-powered engines. They were very new, but they seemed safer than steam engines. Some men had already tried to mount them on bicycles and small carts. Henry thought these men had the right idea.

In 1888, Henry married a young woman named Clara Bryant. His father hoped Henry would settle down as a farmer. His father even gave Henry some land of his own. But the young man did not want to farm the land. He wanted to build engines.

Clara Bryant Ford always believed in Henry. She even helped him with some of his work.

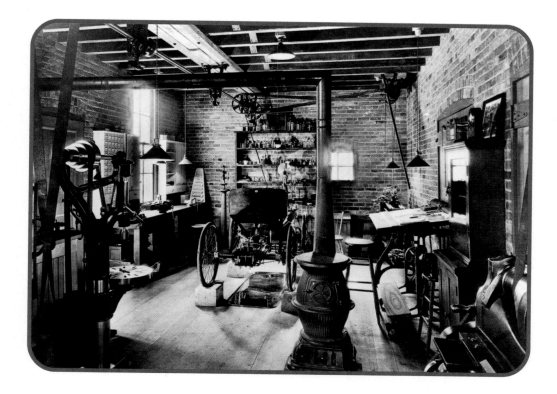

Henry worked on his gas-powered engine in a shop like this one.

Henry liked his work so much that it did not seem like work to him. He tried to build a bicycle engine, but it was too heavy.

Henry wanted to learn more about electricity. He and Clara moved to Detroit. Henry took a job with the electric company.

Chapter 3: Carmaker

Even as a young boy, Edsel Ford shared his father's interest in machines.

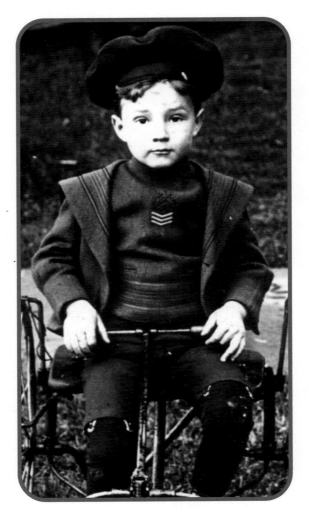

Henry set up a new workshop in Detroit. He spent most of his spare time there. He kept trying to build gas engines. He hoped to use them to run cars or carts of some kind. He worked hard on his ideas. He made friends with other men who were also trying to build gas-powered cars.

The year 1893 was an important one for Henry. Two big events happened in that year. First, Clara had a baby boy. She and Henry named him Edsel. He was the Fords' only child.

The other big event came about on Christmas Eve. That night, one of Henry's engines ran. The engine spit smoke and flame, and then it came to life. Henry was very happy.

The First Ford Car

Of course, this engine was not perfect. Henry kept changing it. He made it run better. Then he started to build a light car for his engine to run. It was slow work, but Henry kept at it. Three years later, he finished his first gas-powered car.

Henry built this car in his workshop. When it was time to test it, the car was too big to fit through the door. Henry had to take down part of a wall to get the car out. After that, the test drive went well.

Henry is shown here with his first car. The horse seems to think the car is strange.

Henry began driving his car around the city. It got plenty of attention. Horses were afraid of it. They had never seen anything like this car. They ran away

when they saw it coming. Most people did not like it, either. They said the car was too noisy. Only a few people seemed to think it might be of use.

Someone offered to pay two hundred dollars for the car. Two hundred dollars was a lot of money back then. Henry took the offer. He put the money to good use. He used it to build his next car.

Starting a Business

In 1899, Henry left his job. He set up his first company. The company built cars that were used to deliver goods. These cars had some problems, and the company did not do well. Henry was sorry when it closed down, but he did not give up. He kept trying to build better cars.

At this time, there were very few cars on the road. They were still quite new. They also cost a lot of money. Only rich people could afford to buy cars.

Even though few people owned cars, car racing was popular. Henry started building race cars. Some of his cars were very fast. They won races. These cars helped Henry make a name for himself. He became known as a man who made good cars.

This is one of Henry's race cars. It was called the "999."

Chapter 4: Force for Change

Henry formed the Ford Motor Company in 1903. This new company built cars. It also gave Henry a chance to work on a new idea. His idea was to build a car that most people could buy and drive. It would sell for a low price. It would be simple and tough.

Henry and his crew began building cars. Their first make was the Model A. It was a good car. But Henry

In 1903, Henry hired dozens of people to build Ford cars.

was not satisfied. He knew he could do better. Over the next few years, he made many changes. He sold many car models. Each one was named for a letter of the alphabet. One was the Model N. One was the Model S.

Building Cars

At first, building cars was slow work. Henry bought parts from **suppliers**. He often had to wait for his parts to be delivered. His workers collected the parts they needed. Only then could they put them together. Working that way, they could build a few cars a day.

Henry saw that the longer it took to build a car, the more the car cost. He did not like that. He wanted his cars to be **affordable**. He wanted more people to buy them.

Henry began to make changes. He stopped buying parts. Instead, he hired workers to make them. He also put in moving belts to carry parts to the workers. These changes cut down the time it took to build a car.

He changed the jobs people did, too. In the past, one worker might build a whole part of a car. Henry thought that took too much time. He told his workers to split up each big job. Each worker did just one task. The belt moved a part from one

Each of these men had one small job to do on each car.

worker to the next. This way was much faster! Soon his workers were building many cars each day.

Henry did not invent most of the methods he used. Others had used them before. But no one had put them together. He was the first. His new system made it easier to build cars and other machines quickly. We now say that he **perfected** a system of **mass production**.

The Model T

Henry did more than change the way people built cars. He also built a car that almost anyone could own. This car was the Model T. It was easy to drive and easy to fix. It was also low priced. It was the car Henry had dreamed of building.

Ford started making Model Ts in 1908. They were a huge hit. Millions of them were sold. By the 1920s, the Model T was the best-selling car in the world.

Before long, horses were almost gone from the streets. Cars and trucks took over. Many of them were Fords. It was a big, big change, and Henry had led the way. His ideas had helped change the world.

Henry and his son, Edsel, posed for this picture in 1928. Of course, the car is a Ford.

Glossary

affordable — low priced

curious — interested in learning more about something

engineer — a person who runs or fixes engines

mass production — quickly making large numbers of parts or machines that are all exactly the same

perfected — made something the best it could be, made perfect

steam engine — an engine that runs on the steam created when water is heated in a boiler

suppliers — people or companies that provide items someone else needs

For More Information

Books

Eat My Dust! Henry Ford's First Race. Monica Kulling
   (Random House)

Henry Ford. Photo-Illustrated Biographies (series). Erika L. Shores
   (Bridgestone)

Story of Model T Fords. Classic Cars (series). David K. Wright
   (Gareth Stevens)

Web Sites

Henry Ford Museum Showroom
www.thehenryford.org/exhibits/showroom/featured.html
Learn about famous cars in history

ThinkQuest: Great Inventors and Inventions
library.thinkquest.org/5847/
Read about Henry Ford and other important inventors

Index

About the Author

Jonatha A. Brown has written several books for children. She lives in Phoenix, Arizona, with her husband and two dogs. If you happen to come by when she isn't at home working on a book, she's probably out riding or visiting with one of her horses. She may be gone for quite a while, so you'd better come back later.